Cougars

by Anne Welsbacher

Consultant:
Christopher M. Papouchis
Conservation Biologist
Mountain Lion Foundation

CAPSTONE
HIGH-INTEREST
BOOKS

an imprint of Capstone Press
Mankato, Minnesota

Capstone High-Interest Books are published by Capstone Press
151 Good Counsel Drive, P.O. Box 669, Mankato, Minnesota 56002
http://www.capstone-press.com

Library of Congress Cataloging-in-Publication Data
Welsbacher, Anne, 1955–
    Cougars/by Anne Welsbacher.
    p. cm.—(Predators in the wild)
    Includes bibliographical references (p. 31) and an index.
    Summary: Describes the physical characteristics, hunting methods, and
distribution of cougars, and their relationship with humans.
    ISBN 0-7368-1316-0 (hardcover)
    1. Puma—Juvenile literature. [1. Puma.] I. Title. II. Series.
QL737.C23 W4463 2003
599.75'24—dc21   2001007913

Editorial Credits

Carrie Braulick, editor; Karen Risch, product planning editor; Timothy Halldin,
    series designer; Gene Bentdahl, book designer and illustrator; Jo Miller, photo
    researcher

Photo Credits

Ann & Rob Simpson, 15
Cheryl A. Ertelt, 9
Comstock, background elements
Corel, 11, 17 (lower left)
Joe McDonald, 6
Joe McDonald/Visuals Unlimited, 16, 22
Kevin Fleming/CORBIS, 29
Leonard Rue Enterprises, 12
Mary Ann McDonald, 8
PhotoDisc, Inc., 17 (upper left, upper right)
Tom & Pat Leeson, 10, 14, 17 (lower right), 18, 20, 27
Tom Walker/Visuals Unlimited, 24
Underwood & Underwood/CORBIS, 28
www.ronkimball/stock.com, cover, 21

1 2 3 4 5 6 07 06 05 04 03 02

Table of Contents

Common names: Cougar, mountain lion, puma, panther, painter

Scientific name: *Puma concolor*

Average size: Most cougars grow 7 to 9 feet (2.1 to 2.7 meters) long from the tips of their tails to their noses. They stand 2 to 3 feet (.6 to .9 meter) tall from the ground to the shoulders.

Average weight: Cougars usually weigh between 75 and 200 pounds (34 and 91 kilograms).

Life span: Cougars live 8 to 10 years.

Habitat: Cougars live in mountains, deserts, grasslands, forests, and swamps.

Prey: Cougars hunt mainly deer. They eat sheep, squirrels, raccoons, rabbits, foxes, skunks, and porcupines. They also eat mice, beavers, coyotes, and birds.

Social habits: Cougars are solitary animals. They live and hunt alone in areas called home ranges.

In This Chapter:

* Cougars have strong legs and muscular bodies.

* Cougars are known by many names.

* Cougars are felids.

Chapter 1

Cougars

Cougars are among the largest predators in North America, South America, and Central America. Only jaguars and bears are bigger. Cougars have powerful legs and strong, muscular bodies to help them hunt prey.

Cougars have many names. People call them mountain lions or cougars in the western United States and in Canada. In the southwestern United States, people call them pumas. In Florida, they are called panthers. People living in the northeastern United States once called cougars catamounts. Other names include painters, mountain screamers, and deer tigers.

Cubs

Cougars mate to produce young. About three months after mating, female cougars give birth to one to six cubs. Cougar cubs are covered with brown or black spots. This spotted pattern helps hide the cubs from predators. The spots fade after about eight months. Female cougars care for their cubs for one to two years.

Species

Cougars are members of the Felidae family. All members of this family are called felids. Felids include both wildcats and domestic cats. Cougars are wildcats. Other wildcats include lions, tigers, jaguars, and bobcats.

Scientists divide families into groups called genera. Cougars are in the genus Puma. Scientists further divide genera into species. Cougars are members of the species *Puma concolor*. Members of a species share certain physical features. *Puma concolor* includes more than 20 cougar subspecies.

Cougars are one of the largest wildcats in North America.

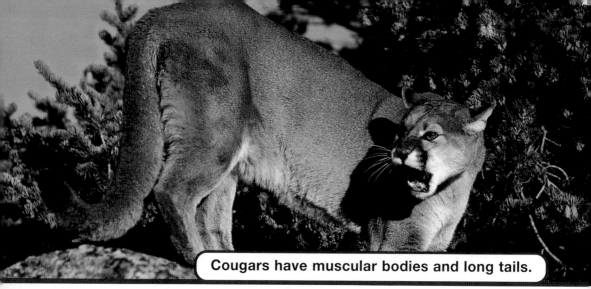

Cougars have muscular bodies and long tails.

Appearance

The cougar has short, thick fur. Its fur is mainly one solid color. This color can range from golden tan to dark brown. Cougars that live in cold climates are a lighter shade than those that live in warm climates.

The cougar has markings. It has a brown or black tip on its tail. The cougar's short, rounded ears have black markings on their back side. The cougar has both black and white facial markings.

Cougars usually grow 7 to 9 feet (2.1 to 2.7 meters) long from the tips of their tails to their noses. They stand 2 to 3 feet (.6 to .9 meter) tall at the shoulders.

Most cougars weigh between 75 and 200 pounds (34 and 91 kilograms). Cougars that live in cold, northern climates usually are larger than cougars in warm, southern climates. The Florida panther is a small subspecies. It weighs between 75 and 80 pounds (34 and 36 kilograms). Some subspecies in Canada can weigh more than 200 pounds.

The cougar has a long tail. A cougar's tail usually is about 2 to 3 feet (.6 to .9 meter) long. A cougar uses its tail to help it balance as it jumps.

A cougar has strong legs with large, padded paws. Its back legs are longer than its front legs. This feature helps the cat leap onto prey.

Home Ranges

Cougars hunt within areas called home ranges. Male cougars may share part of their home ranges with females. But they defend their home ranges from other males.

The size of a cougar's home range often varies according to how much prey is nearby. It may reach across 500 square miles (1,295 square kilometers).

In This Chapter:

* Cougars often hunt near sunrise and sundown.

* Cougars use both vision and hearing to hunt.

* Cougars stalk their prey.

Chapter 2

The Hunt

Cougars are called carnivores because they eat only meat. They hunt mainly deer. They also hunt animals such as squirrels, raccoons, rabbits, foxes, and skunks. Mice, beavers, coyotes, birds, and porcupines also can make up part of their diet.

Most wildcats hunt at night. But cougars hunt during both daylight hours and at night. Cougars often hunt near sunrise and sundown. Deer and other prey often are active during these times.

Cougars can accurately judge their distance from prey.

Senses for Hunting

Cougars use senses to help them locate prey. Their night vision is several times better than that of people. The pupils in their eyes open wide to let in a great deal of light. Cougars cannot see detail as well as people can. But like people, cougars have binocular vision. This type of vision helps them judge distance.

Cougars have good hearing. Scientists believe that cougars can hear high-pitched sounds that people cannot hear.

Tapetum

Cougars have a reflective layer at the back of each eye called a tapetum. The tapetum reflects light back toward the front part of the eye. The eye then can gather light a second time. The tapetum helps cougars hunt in low levels of light.

Cougars crouch low to the ground to stalk prey.

Silent Stalkers

Cougars stalk prey. They walk slowly and quietly so that prey does not notice them. They bend their knees to crouch near the ground. They hide behind rocks, trees, and other objects.

Cougars leap or sprint toward prey when they come near it. They may jump from a high place onto the back of prey. Cougars can jump higher and farther than any other wildcats. They can leap more than 15 feet (4.6 meters) high. They can jump more than 45 feet (14 meters) forward from a still position.

Cougars capture about 80 percent of the prey that they hunt. Many wildcats are not as successful at catching prey. Lions catch about 10 percent of the animals they try to capture. Tigers catch prey even less frequently.

What Cougars Eat

Deer

Foxes

Beavers

Bighorn Sheep

* Cougars kill prey quickly.

* Cougars often cut prey's spinal cord.

* Cougars use their teeth to dig into prey's flesh.

Chapter 3

The Kill

Cougars can kill strong animals much larger than themselves. Some cougars can kill elk that weigh 800 pounds (363 kilograms). Cougars are the only predators living in North America, South America, or Central America that can kill such large animals alone. Other predators hunt large animals in packs.

Quick Killers

Cougars kill prey quickly. They often bite prey near the base of the skull. A cougar has strong jaws and sharp teeth. The cougar's bite often cuts the animal's spinal cord. This thick cord of nerve tissue in the neck and back links the brain to all other nerves. Animals usually die after the spinal cord is cut.

Cougars may kill prey in other ways. They sometimes use their jaws to attack an animal's throat. This action can suffocate prey.

A cougar has two long teeth called incisors at the front of its mouth. The incisors may be as long as 4.5 inches (11 centimeters). They help cougars hold and kill prey by digging into the animal's flesh.

Porcupines

Cougars flip porcupines onto their backs to kill them. The cougars then avoid the porcupine's sharp quills. They attack the porcupine's soft stomach.

Cougars often use their jumping ability to attack prey.

Cougars often jump onto the back of large prey. They grab the prey's head with their paws. They then pull the animal's head back. This action often breaks the animal's neck and spinal cord.

Cougars often drag carcasses long distances before eating them.

Eating Habits

After killing prey, a cougar drags the animal's dead body to a sheltered place such as a cave or a thick area of forest. The cougar tears meat from the carcass to eat. It uses its rough tongue to scrape the bones. An adult cougar may eat as much as 10 pounds (4.5 kilograms) of meat at one time.

Cougars sometimes cache large prey. They bury a carcass that they do not finish eating. They then cover the carcass with twigs, leaves, dirt, or snow. They return to eat more of the body later. A large carcass can supply a cougar with food for one week.

Cougars do not always finish eating a carcass. They may leave a carcass if the meat begins to rot.

Myth versus Fact

Myth: Cougars can be easily tamed and kept as pets.

Fact: Cougars are wild animals. They are dangerous to keep as pets.

Myth: Cougars are cowardly.

Fact: A cougar will risk its life to catch a large animal. Cougars hunt large moose, elk, and bighorn sheep. The sharp horns on these animals could easily kill them.

Myth: Cougars often hunt livestock.

Fact: Cougars rarely hunt livestock unless other prey is hard to find.

In This Chapter:

* Cougars have a large range.

* Many cougars starved during the 1800s.

* People continue to move into cougar habitats.

n the World of People

Cougars have a large range. They live in the western parts of Canada and the United States. They live throughout Central and South America. Cougars called Florida panthers live in southeastern Florida.

Cougars live in a variety of habitats. They live in forests, mountains, and deserts. Their habitat also includes jungles, grasslands, and swamps.

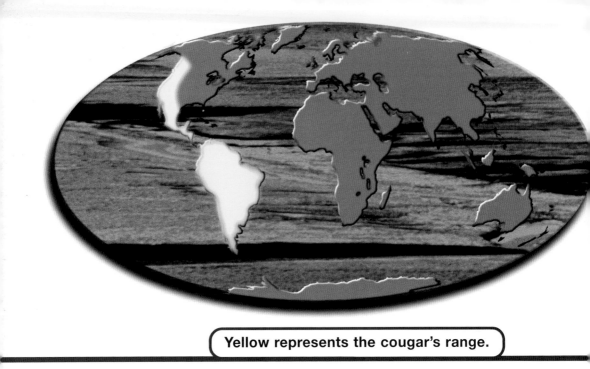

Yellow represents the cougar's range.

Decreasing Range

The cougar's range is smaller than it was in the past. Cougars once lived throughout the United States. More than 2,000 panthers once lived in Florida. Today, only 30 to 50 panthers remain. Some cougar subspecies in Canada are in danger of dying out.

The cougar's range has shrunk for many reasons. In the 1600s, Europeans began to settle the eastern United States. These people feared cougars. They thought the animals would kill their livestock. The early settlers hunted and killed thousands of cougars. They also built roads, homes, and buildings in cougar habitats.

In the 1800s, people hunted and killed many deer for meat. Few deer were available for cougars to eat. Many cougars starved. People also continued to hunt cougars. The cats died out in some areas.

Cougar Attacks

Cougars usually avoid people. People rarely see them in the wild. But cougars may attack people. In the 1990s, there were 53 reported cougar attacks in North America.

The number of cougar attacks has been increasing throughout the past several years. People have been moving into cougar habitats as they build homes and buildings in wilderness areas.

Habits

Cougars share many habits with small domestic cats. They hiss and purr. They groom their fur and crouch while eating. Cougars also sharpen their claws on objects as domestic cats do.

The Future of Cougars

People began to work to save cougars in the mid-1950s. They passed laws to make hunting illegal in areas with low cougar populations. They established protected areas for the wildcats.

In Florida, people are working to increase cougar populations in several ways. Some people raise young cougars and release them into the wild. Workers have built special paths which allow cougars to walk under roadways instead of across them. Scientists sometimes catch sick cougars and give them medicine.

Today, scientists are not certain how many cougars live in the wild. Cougar populations are increasing

Cougar Beliefs

American Indians held various beliefs about cougars. Many tribes respected cougars' excellent hunting ability. Some American Indians honored cougars. A few tribes killed them. But cougars were not hunted in large numbers until Europeans settled in North America.

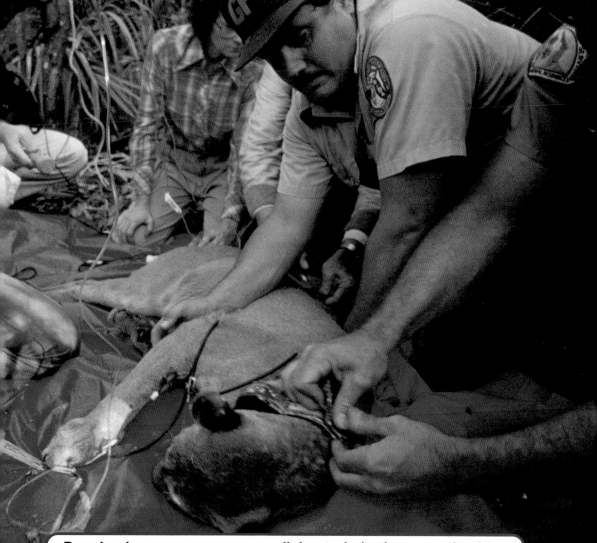

People give some cougars medicine to help them stay healthy.

in some areas. The largest cougar population lives in western Canada. Habitat loss is the largest threat to the survival of cougars. Efforts are needed to protect cougars as people continue to move into cougar habitats.

cache (KASH)—to hide or store for later use

carcass (KAR-kuhss)—the body of a dead animal

carnivore (KAR-nuh-vor)—an animal that eats meat

domestic (duh-MESS-tik)—no longer wild; people keep domestic animals as pets or for food.

habitat (HAB-uh-tat)—the place and natural conditions in which a plant or animal lives

incisors (in-SY-zurs)—long, sharp teeth near the front of the mouth; incisors help cougars tear into prey.

spinal cord (SPY-nuhl KORD)—a thick cord of nerve tissue in the neck and back; the spinal cord links the brain to the body's other nerves.

stalk (STAWK)—to hunt an animal in a quiet, secret way

tapetum (tuh-PEE-tuhm)—layer of membranes at the back of the eye; the tapetum reflects light toward the front of the eye.

To Learn More

Gouck, Maura. *Mountain Lions.* Nature Books. Chanhassen, Minn.: Child's World, 2001.

Hodge, Deborah. *Wild Cats: Cougars, Bobcats, and Lynx.* Wildlife. Buffalo, N.Y.: Kids Can Press, 1999.

Middleton, Don. *Pumas.* Big Cats. New York: PowerKids Press, 1999.

Wrobel, Scott. *Mountain Lions.* Northern Trek. Mankato, Minn.: Smart Apple Media, 2000.

Useful Addresses

Canadian Wildlife Service
Environment Canada
Ottawa, ON K1A 0H3

Florida Panther Society
Route 1, Box 1895
White Springs, FL 32096

Eastern Cougar Foundation
P.O. Box 91
North Springs, WV 24869

Mountain Lion Foundation
P.O. Box 1896
Sacramento, CA 95812

Internet Sites

Cat Specialist Group

http://lynx.uio.no/catfolk

Mountain Lion Foundation Kids Page

http://www.mountainlion.org/Kids/kids.htm

Wild about Cats

http://wildaboutcats.org

Index